stoned words& electric flowers

Jerry Palmer

volume 3

ISBN 979-8-3484-6935-1
First Printing 2024

Written from 1972-2024
Designed in Sublette County, Wyoming
Printed in Rankin County, Mississippi
Cover uses Cooper Black and Cooper Nouveau typefaces
Body uses Minion Pro and the Cooper Nouveau typefaces

All images appearing in this book are courtesy of the Palmer Family Archives.

Paint Bucket Brigade Publishing
Rankin County, Mississippi

jerrypalmerauthor.com

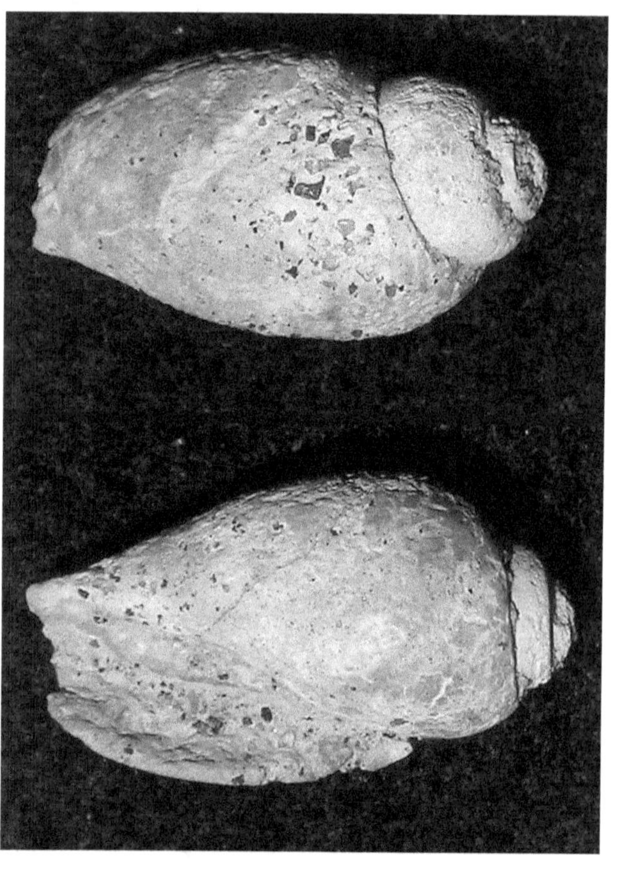

Lines Of Time

Nite before all was fine - till You found.
You're not the only one in line.
Thinking of what You told me years ago.
No matter how long I tried,
You were forever to be by my side.
Don't want the peaches… Don't shake the tree.
Games of the mind… Games of the soul.
Tell me dear one, what secrets do You hold?
Ashes to Ashes… Dust to Dust
Words to Words… so as my trust
did You sweep away.
As it were a speck of lent or a piece of rust.
The eyes of children can see
the world spinning round.
Turning night into day with the sun rising
when later going down.
All the music seems but busy sounds, laughter,
and tears.
Causing hopes and fears, be sure in
Your mind of the years.
We traveled being far apart yet always with a sense
You were near
As we cast our hearts with the ties that bind
to the lines of time.

Dead Pines

Dead pines by a dry pond with one last duck.
Wishing for rain but no such luck.
Trees yet to grow with seeds covered in mud,
longing for spring or perhaps frost.
Just a sign that all isn't lost.
Once was told care not for, they're just trees
the limbs will fall, and the wood will rot.
This couldn't be further from the truth, yet not a lie.
Unless one hasn't climbed into the branches
to touch the sky.
Or touched the leaves with their face.
Having stepped out on a limb while holding
another tight.
Always use three points on a climb,
know your equipment
while looking around and studying the vines.
Be it the birds, lichens, moss or the bark,
trees are full of life.
Keeping things grounded and offering places
for those in flight.
Even after it falls the logs enrich life for creatures
big and small.

Old Growth Trees

Can't say where I saw one last,
perhaps at Sky Lake or Cypress Swamp.
Most of what is there now are snags
and a few stumps.
Or perhaps in Brandon,
that Sycamore tree off Highway 80.
A few old Cedars lost in the woods
or the Oak in Lena,
which fell causing flooding
and a lot of no good.
Big Pines are short timers at best,
the drought started it all.
Pine beetles and their friends did the rest.
Relics of the past grew and flourished,
before saws were powered by gas.
Most folks will never know for there is little to show,
How huge these trees where and how their canopies
sheltered life below.
Sassafras, Dogwoods, Elms, Post Oaks,
and others of their kind
need our favor while there is still time.

Green Parrot

Last seen flying above Preston Road,
headed north where it is sure to be cold.
Parrot or Macaw, pet shop breakout
or escape from the cage on the patio.
No one knows and no one sees that
in the fall when the world is so small,
winds from the Arctic can reach into
Texas with nothing to slow the chill,
Save the small trees that try but never will.
Bend Trees north of town lean to the left
yet never touching the ground.
From the Post Oaks to the Mesquite thickets
and back to Pecans along the creeks.
Flies this lost bird wanting only to be home
in the vines of the jungle or near the cliffs
where they gathered only to be trapped
and hauled away.
None for better all for the worse, marketing
these animals for a dollar.

Still the Americans buy and still the
small children cry,

For the lost parrot in the sky.

LYCORIS ROSE
GARDEN
EST. 2005
AND INTO
THE
Garden
I go
TO LOSE
MY
MIND
and find
my soul
INTERNATIONAL
OPEN WATER
DIVER
The diver identified on the reverse side has satis-
factorily completed the required training skills in a
course of diving as set forth by the Professional
Association of Diving Instructors
PADI
INTERNATIONAL
PROFESSIONAL ASSOCIATION
OF DIVING INSTRUCTORS

Games Played & Price Paid

Games on paper - games with lights, are these games of nature, or merely games of fright?

Questions of life, the tolls and of the price, more questions of health vs. wealth.

Such as which air to breathe, what to take with us, what or who do we leave?

Are we alone with these questions of doubt, or will Mother Nature cast us out?

Hearing her siren songs, can we heal the wounds merely with flowers that bloom?

Some will listen thus joining the chorus, others continue the path of doom.

Beating the drums in hopes of saving themselves for kingdom come.

Better to be last instead of first in the games we play,

Yet it is said, lead, follow or get the hell out of the way.

No Wind... No Air

Towers of sand melted into glass from bombs
in the desert.
Made in a moment of time – to last longer than we
have been around.
Patterns formed years before, tools of war forever
bear our mark.
Equals profits for many as we burn the sun,
Wondering why it's so hot with the earth on fire?
Peace has been shallow & very murky.
Visions short sighted, often mistaken dreams at best.
Progress will forever bear our mark which we
reached without much reward.
Except save those with plunder in the heart.
Robbing the people as you fed the poor, drill, drill & drill.
Always having a barrel to fill.
Causes are many, reasons number even more.
Some stood in the way, others barricaded the doors.
Waving wooden swords hiding as signs, never
bothered them much.
Time has let it be shown, most of what was warned
has come about.
Save the ideas that began to stir the wind & filter the air.
Where acorns & seeds were sown, now woodlots
with gardens grow.
While believers plant & continue to say, just wait, it'll
be a better day.

During the Dry Days of the Drought of 2023

Summer heat as never before or at least since
Santorio built thermometers.
Rains with no drops just sheets of vapor in the air,
sunshine like fire reaching
out then consuming all that is there.
Trees brown from the drought, me watering small
shrubs like it's gonna count.
Planting again without water is like saying something
without opening your mouth.
Watch what grows without our help then nurture
these plants by leaving them alone.
If you must do something, compost everything
that has lived,
Then watch the seeds sprout on their own & grow
in the sidewalks.
Grow in the streets, grow in the planters,
grow beneath our feet.

When you realize heart & earth are both of the same letters, it all begins to make sense.

Mother Nature is Mad

Pages of tears will remain for years.
Do we ruin Mother Nature just to be clever?
Moved the river, burned the forest,
took a dozer to the land.
Move more people, mostly those in the way.
Never ready learned to share; cause that ain't the
American way.
Unless there is something to gain & then
we're on the way.
For the falsehoods result in tears, the waste is forever.
The waters seem to carry it away downstream,
where others live & others dream.
Not just a creek or just a stream, all are connected,
all flow together.
As the rivers rise so be our cries of Clean Water,
Clean Air if not for the sons,
surely for the daughters as their connection
is greater and should be heard,
Mother Nature is mad, and her justice will be had.

Magic Fields

Magic could seem endless if not for time
getting in the mix.
Who walks all passages, swims all seas,
and crawls all tunnels.
Why do we ask much less expect answers,
for there are those that always know.
As there are those who wonder and wander
without ever getting lost.
While those among us who draw, paint, garden,
or work with their hands.
Can only wonder as the thunder crashes
after the lightning strikes,
Rain falls over the fields where the magic grows,
will there be a crop?
Only time will tell if the conditions are there,
and mycelium grew from the spores
that move in the air.
The planet is magic as everything is connected
from the bottom to the top.
Shared these things and the future became the past,
walked the fields looking for jewels among the grass.

Oil of Soil

Oil from the plants is what they said, algae
and ferns under pressure.
Came this mess in which we swim, not very clean
but makes a pretty sheen.
What's going on – building more
than we need – is only greed.
Can I say what is wrong and only what is right?
Only seeing wrongs will shape half-truths
among the most earnest of souls.
The sun shines freely, often hot to the touch.
Its glory hides behind clouds, its brightness
shouts out loud.
Sunshine grows the plants, which clean the air.
Will the uses be fruitful, or will we act as
if it's not there?
Solar covers the planet off & on every day.
Older than life, new as of today.
Turn off the Nukes & turn on the Sun.
Oil all over the soil, must be another way.

Candles by the Wall

Candles to melt – do little else – but pretty to see.
Colors are as bright as the leaves on the trees, just
before they fall.
Stones of music, stones of rock, stones of concrete,
stones of art…
Heard them all now, they've built a wall – which
seems rather small.
Questions of how long & how tall, made of what,
plus put it where?
Across someone's backyard, into the garden then
down by dry creek.
Made of mud or out of sticks, perhaps out of steel.
Knowing some will crumble, others just gonna rust.
Wonder why they come, where will they go?
To roof the houses & help the gardens grow
& bury the cables.
So, we can watch the tv show.
Dust from the road fills their hair, cuts from the wire
burn the skin.
All to get here & start again, leaving family,
leaving friends.
Wanting to stay but having to go.
Would you leave to provide for yours,
if the threat was so bad,
and this journey was the only hope you had?

Buy A Landscape

Buy a landscape, grow a garden,
both will work the fool out of you.
Looking at plans of circles and squares, not knowing
one plant from another is usually how it goes.
You could leave the dirt & trees alone,
giving the roots respect & the birds a home.
No need to haul the soil away only to buy it back
another day.
Same with the plants, learn the flora & their needs.
Find the bare spots, mulch, or sow native seeds.
Collect seeds from the roadside flowers in late
summer through fall.
Let them dry then label, then sow before it rains if
you are so lucky.
Or wonder when the landscape crew will appear?
Is it too wet or did they just have a bigger job
close to here?
Can't get the plants from the nursery
or the irrigation is broken
again, with no rain in sight.
The drainage is bad & this only will get worst
cause water wouldn't run uphill unless it's the big
pipe that burst.

Primordial Soup Recipe

One moon seems so far away,
stars so close that they can be seen in the day.
Hollow yet whole, solid but able to bend.
Wood to ashes – Ore to metal – Sand to glass
Ashes to dust – Metal to rust – Glass to beads
Then to powder stir it slowly,
try not to kick up any dust.
Mix with leaves, manure & table scraps
with a bash of charcoal.
Now add rainwater gathered during
a lightning storm.
Plus, a handful of Moss, sit it in the shade
on the stack of stone.
Watch Nature unfold; not to worry this mix
can yield stories untold.
Of the garden ferns, dragonflies, earthworms,
centipedes, and moles.
Dust again begins to settle, for from
across the ocean it blows.
Now settled upon the soup of time,
the water turns green
thus begins the dream…

Sharp Water

Glass so sharp to the touch much too sharp to hold.
Like a bottle thrown out the window crashing
on the road.
Cut my soul like an old page – made the cut
– then the fold.
Always was told; after I was born,
they broke the mold.

… & …

The mist of winter is the whisper of trees.
Miles slow or fast, add to the years as wood
adds to splinters.
Crossroads appear more often in a world
grown small.
Reach for what you desire, stretch early
cause you might have to reach higher.
In the land of seasons, it's the mist of winter.
That gather on the leaves of trees causing dewdrops
to fall as rain, upon the ground needing to soak in
starting the cycle again.

I burn with love for
revolution & social justice
Mutual Aid
Self-defense
Public education
Care / Listening
L'Éclatante
Revolutionary matches
ALL CATS ARE BEAUTIFUL
Direct Action
Occupation
Strikes
Sabotage
All against oppressions

January 7, 1980

Cold and sunny on this January day, wonder how it
was 70* yesterday.
Friends in jail for climbing a fence, told the judge it
was self-defense.
50 days behind bars - refusing to pay the fine.
 She stood for earth then crossed the line.
They need a deep dark hole to bury the waste, sealed
in concrete,
partially hidden, permanently poison.
CPLF tried to hold the light hoping others would
enter the fight.
Hiking at night, carrying a little water, never a torch.
No flames, no weapons, hiding in the cactus,
Feeling the passion of struggle justified
in the souls around.
Signs and tools, words and fools.
Doing what we can just to save the land.

CAN'T HUG
YOUR KIDS
WITH
NUCLEAR ARMS!

Direct Action

Fight the lines, fight the fines $$
Fight with all resources, fight at all times.
Like running in the woods, then tripping
on the vines.
Know you're gonna fall; gotta get up
there's more to do.
Post-occupation blues has its' on medicine.
Planning the next action and trusting in You.

…&…

Lichens on the rocks
Peat moss from the ground
Algae in the water
Spanish moss in the Cypress
Ball moss in the Live Oaks
Ferns on the riverbanks
Resurrection fern on the Post Oak
Osage Orange grown for fences,
horse high, bull strong & pig tight.

Light Sand

Rumors of who you know, more about
who you knew.
Walked down most trails, down some you run.
Stand not long in the shifting sands.
So not to lose those shoes.
So not to get the blues.
Keep moving your toes as the sand comes around.
This is what I found – of the many colors.
Of the many shades – the ones I favored.
Were the dark & the grays
Sad in the morning – sleepy in the nite?
Sun shines in the morning & stars reflect it at nite.
Hard to write, harder to read.
Doesn't really matter, just filling a need.
Avoiding going to jail, some didn't, and some will.
Do what you must, do what you feel.
Gotta do something, tired of sitting still.

M-16 or AK-47

Walkin down the trail knowing you cannot fail.
Gotta win today for the fight is here to stay.
Dead in the ditch, dead in the booth.
Don't vote for them, you know it's no use!
Reds in the jungle, reds in the street.
Red is our blood when the bullets meet.
Stop the Guns!!
Stop the War!!!
Let there be Peace tomorrow.
Give me the shells.
Give me the guns.
Send them all to hell, just for fun.

Clouds of Seeded Rain
or is it Smoke?

Drawing in ink helps me think of what
I'm not sure about.
It doesn't really matter like I said before.
You don't have to be crazy, You don't have to be sane.
To know if it's raining or if it's just water on the brain.
Can't help the masses if You can't help yourself.
Can't read a book if it's left on the shelf.
This time of action, that time of foe.
If we don't speak up – how will others ever know?
Smoke rises filling the sky, woods are burning
more every day.
Little critters can't run if there's no place to go.
Waters have boiled away now the fires
in Australia are here to stay.
Weather patterns have shifted faster,
than the continents have drifted.
The mountain still burns today,
after nearly 6,000 years.
Coal for the stove, coal for the furnace,
coal burns in the earth.
So, Nature gives & Nature takes away.
Tribesman set the fire to keep others
from coming near.
So, the fire burns & smoke rises filling the sky.
Wanted to make clouds, needing them to cry.

Green Rose
Colonial Country Club
ANTIQUE ROSE EMPORIUM
9300 Lueckemeyer Rd. Brenham, TX 77833
(979) 836-9051

Green

Plants in the garden – plants in the sea – plants give
us our breath.
Green is the color that lets us be & the largest
is just a tree.
Growing all around yet in many places few are found.
Green is of many shades, with these in the eyes
of the beholder.
For life to be so short & we're always on the run.
Green grows, some is eaten, a lot is mowed.
Learn to smell the roses & other beauties You see.
Green breaks up the sidewalk & can bring
down a house.
Just look around hopefully something fragrant
sprouts out of the ground.
Green only lasts a couple of months or perhaps
several hundred years.
Yet sooner or later it all turns brown.
Green are the plants & the envy in me.
Green is the coolest color You'll ever see.

Tree Damage

Torn not to heal, broken in a way not to be glued.
Lost the way, never to be found.
Gone are a number of challenges which
blocked the path.
Need to slow down wanting the dream to last.
Toiled in the soil with dirt under my nails.
Torn the skin with briars & thorns, cut holes
in the leather gloves.
Hot knife through butter is what they say.
Can't walk by a rose without giving blood away.
Not knowing any better or caring in the least,
How can we change if all act like beasts?
Wounds will heal unless it's a tree, these grow over.
Trees cannot heal as we do, they make no repairs.
They defend themselves by growing a wall.
Never mind the cause, they compartmentalize.
Kinda like this country if you think about it at all.

Coyote Runs

Cries in the nite, cries in the rain & cries in the dark.
Yet no one knows their names.
Ask no questions, hear no tales, walk very quietly.
Gotta be ready to run like hell.
Howls in the nite, howls in the rain
& howls in the darkness.
Makes for runs only Coyotes can explain.
Never in any cactus yet always in a rush & trying to
stop the madness.
Knowing there are others out there yet
trusting only us.
Maybe the reason for cries in the nite,
howls in the rain.
Wanting to hear tales & have someone explain
why we are so shallow?
As not to feel or care for the earth beneath
our feet leaving but a shadow.
Some do plant, most just rant,
wanting to reap the harvest.
Without ever sowing a seed, without having a stance.
Time on this earth, time in this space, brief are the
moments of change.
No words can help when you're alone,
breath in, breath out.
Howl in the nite & cry in the rain…

Dennis Banks

Ran thru the years, ran your own Trail of Tears.
Gone to jail today, hope you can walk away.
Acts of justice never receive praise, lost in the ways,
you're fighting to save from Alcatraz
to Robeson County
Time and lies form a thick haze,
from Yellow Thunder.
No news to be heard – from Aim not a word.
Ghost dancers come to mind,
cross the plains of buffalo grass.
Into in sands of time… resist the waters
and be carried away.
Hit and run, to fight another day.
Hide in plain sight, plant trees & grasses,
take time as a weapon.
Use it wisely or the best you can, for there is no map.
Much less a plan… there were leaders before,
there will be leaders again.
Standing Rock to Wounded Knee…
George Floyd to Rankin County.

MISSISSIPPI
LYCORIS
03 RANKIN

Flower Mound Trees

Times of the future, look back at me from the past.
Words written from actions taken,
some forgotten in the rage.
Seem more like a ghost – gone are the stones
now turned to dust.
Even the steel blades have begun to rust.
Used to cut limbs in dead wooden trees,
Live Oaks & Bodark
Climb in my dreams, always tied in
from the highest point.
Work in the air held by a rope with
or without a joint.
Shovels with broken handles have dug many a tree.
Balled and bur lapped after being dug by hand,
not many have this skill… perhaps the children will.

Tree a Day

North Haven Gardens with three crews
landscaped Dallas,
from Turtle Creek to White Rock Lake.
Removing the old plants mostly tossing them away.
Learned the skills to work for the wealthy
and still get paid.
Ask no questions and you'll hear mostly lies.
Architects drew the plans, sold the jobs, picked the
plants, got the credit.
So, it's fair to say, they never stuck a shovel
into the black clay.

Road Work

Need a road so we don't get stuck,
using a wheelbarrow instead of a truck.
Starting in 1988, used a rock hammer,
a hit of windowpane and a broken plate.
Used old bricks, new bricks, found stone
and golf balls from the lakes.
Waves in the water hitting the shore,
dove for the trinkets.
Always hoping to find more, looked in places
I have never been.
Learned in jail all could fail if it's anger
without a cause.
Years to reflect having taken a cause to heart.
Can't begin the change without a running start.
Can't fuss at others for the things you still do.
Reuse the rubble and built a road,
it maybe not be level,

yet it can carry a load, be it a wheelbarrow
or a pickup truck.
Waste with the haste in which we live,
has wounded the Earth.
This you can feel as you look for the forest,
seeing only trees.
This you can see as you look at all the trash
in the streams.
This you can see as you look at the rusty tractors
still in the fields.
Compost everything as you go along the way
or just let it be.
If you're looking for answers,
buy a shovel & plant some trees.
Or get a pick & a rock hammer & knee pads
& come see me.

Working the Dirt

Learned this early now it's too late,
some get to choose,
for others it's just fate with a twist of time.
From bean fields to the pine trees farms.
None can rest or even fold their arms.
Can't just sit at a desk writing the checks.
Hoping nothing breaks or it rains before bailing hay.
No help without the kids yet they gotta be fed,
then put to bed.
Back to plowing the fields after clearing the stumps.
Keep digging the well cause there ain't no pumps.
Living in the woods, this is what you do.
Cockfights on Saturday, church on Sunday hoping
for forgiveness for gambling away the money.
Stills flow in a dry county, clubs by the river
help ease the fever.
Many have gone trapping for a mink, fox,
or a few beavers.
Selling the pelts makes a few coins feel like wealth.
Note on the farm is due, cow is dry
& the kids got the flu.
No doctor in town, no one else around.
Maybe the Granny Woman will know what to do.

Little Trees

He walked the land searching for goodness,
carrying a seedling in his hand.
Stopping by a stream – grazing into the water
catching a glimpse of the goodness he longed for.
Plus, a hard look at tomorrow.
The tree he planted had grown to the strongest
and wisest in the forest.
Giving life – caring for life, shedding leaves
to the wind.
Shade in the summer for strangers
– resting spot for rangers.
Live Oak, Pecan or Osage Orange
he never was to know.
Just a tree by the stream of life as winters
come and go.
In looking into the stream - being glad
there was still water moving.
Summers were burning yet the precious water
flow onward.
Toward the gulf marking a path
for the Whopping Cranes, Monarchs
and other souls with wings.
It was time for him to go, having planted the twig.
Into this great tree did it grow, budding in Spring
sleeping when it snowed.

Dead Trees... 2023

The trees were on fire without any flame, no rain
became the blame.
Watched as one or two faded then
the whole woodlot began to pay.
Green pines in July had been fried on the stump,
couldn't stop it as they began to die.
Now in December all you can do is wonder
at their glory.
Pines, Magnolias and Cryptomeria, all evergreens,
all toast.
Some planted with a shovel, some volunteered
from the seed bank.
Whether or not is the choice you make,
plant the trees to cool the sky.
This is what we can do, you and I.
It's really an honor to plant in the earth,
all should try.

Hoping to stand in the shade of a grove,
watching wings of young birds unfold.
More Oaks are needed, acorns abound to be seeded.
Magnolias & Beech are part of the southern forest,
Black Cherry, White Oak, Hickory
along with a Hackberry tree.
Many were cut and split into firewood
as many were into fence posts.
Few still stand as sentinels as the barbed wire rust,
stapled into time.
Wondering what more to do other than plant trees,
Mulch after watering, praising the leaves,
for they feed the soil along with my soul.

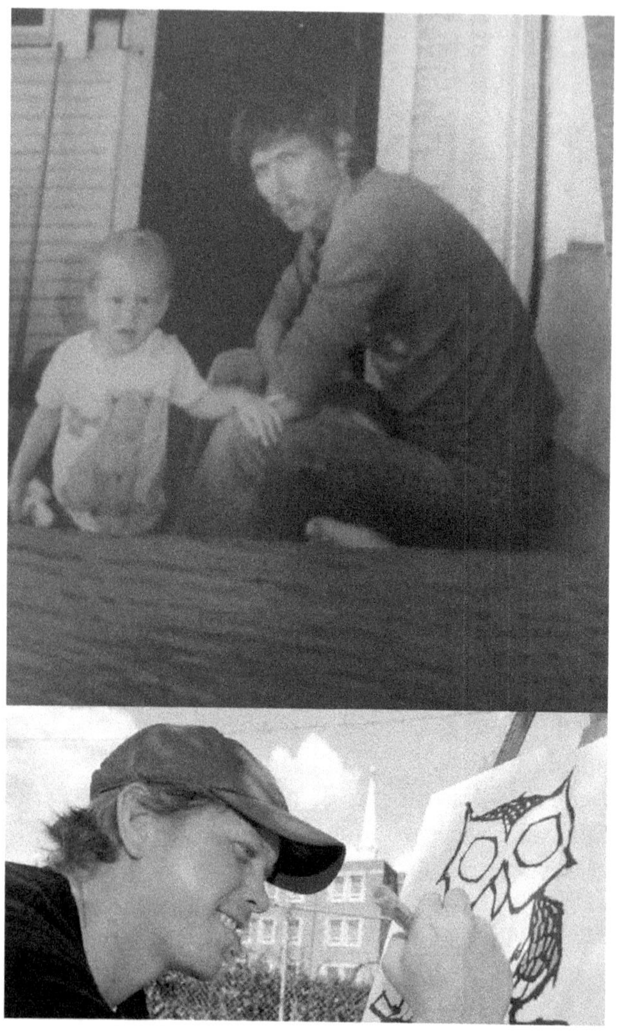

It's Been a Minute

A few blank pages but no blank time,
no other option makes them rhyme.
Here my author glasses help me focus,
on words written not to be heard.
Seeing the writing not hearing a word,
lost to the pages bound in the three.
Stoned Words & Electric Flowers,
colored by Shawn, written by me.

Make ♥
Not War.

Retired Pots

Making tires into pots then those into planters.
Planters to the people at the craft fairs of the day.
Retired pots seem to make them smile, art from tires.
That traveled for the miles in the road or in the yard.
Cut, flip and paint – cut, flip and paint.
Two arts shows and a Day in the Country,
Chapel of The Cross.
From the Courthouse in Vicksburg
where I met Laurie Parker.
Artist, poet, and Lady of Woe, cast a light upon me,
Tho she was never to know, years later
gave her the photo
of her booth and the light, it did show.
Carrying the books for years, caring not for the fame.
Shy it seems, yet all who know her praise her name.
Planting bulbs and other things,
wanted to be remembered.
Flipped tires for a while, guaranteed not to break.
Marked with a hog ring knowing
these were mine, make no mistake.

Painting the Roses Red

Painting the roses red, now Lady Di is dead.
After bringing the monarch to his knees.
Just a light in our time of darkness,
this candle in the wind.
Many have praised her and rightfully so,
blessed to have shared this time.
Quick to the race always moving setting the pace.
Charles in his garden with another woman
you know.
Even if the roses were pink, one must ponder,
one must think.
Desertion of this flower whom we will see no more.
How cold it must be to have blood of royalty.
Althorp has an island upon which she rests –
all will envy - none will best.
Not that he loved her, not that she cared.
All the rumors throughout the years.
The boys are grown and the crown of thrones
he now owns.
Her time was not long in this place.
Like roses we have cut and placed in a vase.
Time crumbles the petals, still painting the roses red.
Lady Di is dead… August 31,1997

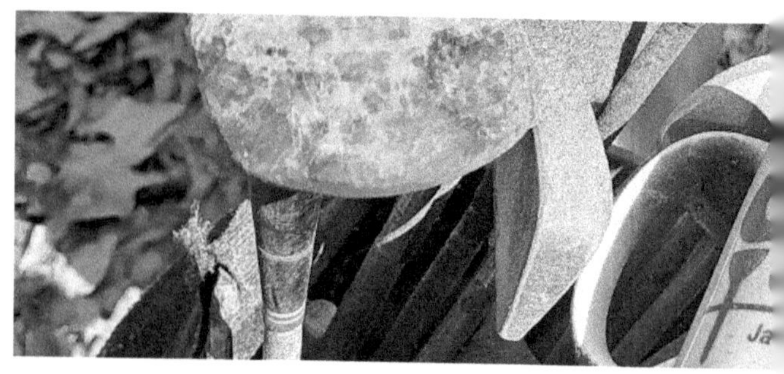

Lighter Knots

The year 1999 arrived just in time,
Charlie -master wooden boat builder came to visit.
98's fireworks were so clear, lots of color
and cost so dear.
Shawn is now a senior – riding the road
paying for his truck.
Hope it holds together and no one gets stuck.
Garden in the day, on Tuesdays get the pay.
Onward to the future – staying this way.
Mulching the bare spots trying to grow some green.
If this keeps going – it'll turn out to be
as good as it seems.
Golfers don't care, they don't give a hoot.
If the greens are toxic and the water, you can't drink.
All that matters is finding the ball
and the next putt they sink.
Bottle rockets by the dozen, firecrackers by the score.

Mortars sound the best, yet a flair gun
put them all to rest.
Smoke in the grass from a fuse which didn't burn.
Wait until tomorrow or a hot hard lesson
you could learn.
No shells in the fire only beer bottles
and an occasional aerosol can.
Toss it in and run while you can.
The fire pit burns bright with lighter knots, pine tops,
a few logs plus and an occasional cardboard box.
Ask me no question and I'll tell you no lies,
Truth is burning pine is tough on the eyes.

We can't just vote fascism away, the time has come to DISOBEY
(be brave!)

ELF... Earth Liberation Front

Doing the burn- making them hurt.
Which is better – which is worse?
Cutting the trees or making a road?
All for the tourists & the gold they hold.
Or leaving it alone for birds to fly
and wolves to roam.
Not much to do once it's gone.
Burnt the lodge turned it to ashes, sabotaging the lift.
Melt the steel, make it hurt.
Save the Earth – while she can still feel.
What a lofty vision, like standing in an ant hill.
Being barefoot walking on stones, Earth will be ok.
Ten thousand years after we go away.
Years of wasting both time and materials,
all bids are out.
Will you hear our shout?
We're doing the burn; will you ever learn?
Stripping the planet or carving the crush.
Wood to ashes, iron to rust.
Backwards we must go so the children will know.

...$$$...

Earth Liberation Front… thanks for trying.

NO
TRUCKS

Hurt the Machine!!!

Break all the glass and turn it back to sand.
Bring all the stones from the walls that fell.
Cause this just got started and it's gonna go on.
Atlatl or bow, slingshot, or hoe, gotta do something.
Ate all the seed corn and now wouldn't you know.
The season is right but there are no seeds to sow.
Hurt the machine, melt the wires.
Cut thru the cage, break all the gauges,
flatten the tires.
Remove all the hoses, drain all the tanks,
do all you dare.
Yet be very aware and try not to be like those at
Tiananmen Square.
They don't care for you much less want you there.
Hit and run, say it loud then go away.
Always making mental notes, hiding in plain sight.
Making them realize even the smallest fire ant
has quite a bite.
Do all you can – then plant a tree or two.
One in the front seat, one in the back…
If you have any left, plant some in the tracks.

January 2, 1999

Cost of Doing Business

Drill and nail, metal or ceramic
makes them take care.
All logs are screened, makes it expensive and the
sawyers beware.
Ruin the blades on the bar or at the mill,
the cost is high for the old growth they kill.
Hammer and spike…
One for owls, two for the wolves, three for the turtles.
Four for the mice, five for the stumps they cooked,
Heart pine then turpentine, nothing left to do.
But move along and destroy something new.
Railroad spurs are scars that will last
till a dozer cuts another path.
Getting to the last cypress back in the swamp.
Cut and haul leaving only the stump.

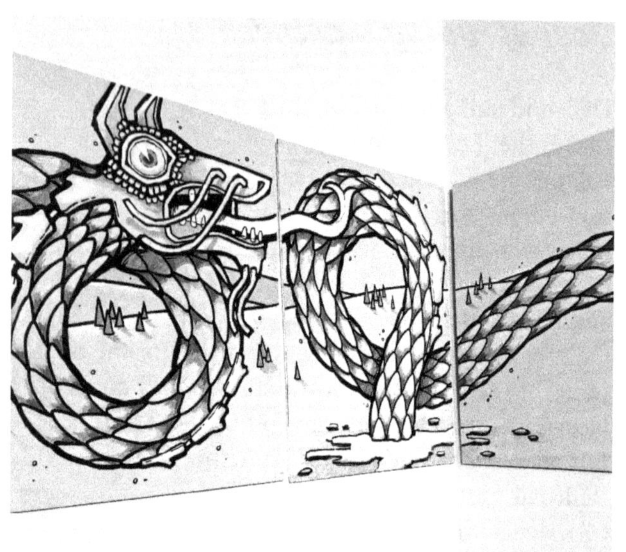

Run Away Look

Things had to get better, so that's why you left.
Your comic book heroes let you down, so it's time to
find another town.
No matter where you roam – most places
will remind you of home.
Look not behind – nothing there but a waste of time.
I won't say anymore – but I ask –
why do you live your life like it's a chore?
Are things any clearer shown
when you're rich in years?
Spilled all the tears like a stream flowing downhill.
If we don't know now, we probably never will.
That life is a long bumpy road,
and each day is another hill.
You gotta plant the roses which later you can smell.
Gotta put in the work or just run away.
Look around before you go, ask those in line,
if all this is worth your time?
Some will say yes, some will say no.
Either way face it as an adventure,
enjoy where you go.

Dear Lady Jane

The years have gone faster than
you would have liked.
But the memories are forever
because we know what it was like.
Playing in the yard, playing red rover
with cousins and friends.
Walking down the gravel road
not knowing the distance.
Or the mysteries it would hold.
Seeing you again made me realize
all roads either keep going
in circles tho some never seem to bend.
From fish fries to watching comets go by.
To Memphis where journeys wind down,
and others began.
The Wolf River flows tight around the trees
while slowly thru the cypress knees.
If the moments in time were diamonds on a string.
Yours would be a tiara of opals for you are truly one
of a kind.

Kayak Trees with Water Knees

This may be hard to believe when it comes from me.
I fell into a crystal ball thus could walk across the sea.
Seeing fish in the water and the gulls
around the shore.
Wanting the shells, I couldn't touch anymore.
The wind caught my bubble, the waves did it toss.
From one shore to the other never seemed
to stay lost.
Into a cypress swamp did I float,
hanging moss dressed the trees.
All around the ancient ones rose wooden barriers
we call knees.
Wonder about their reason, wonder is this
how they breathe?
Escaping the saws of yesterday and standing
thru the storms of today.
The winds again caught my vessels
causing the bubble to pop.
Into the primordial soup I did drop,
only turtles and gators to guide the way,
water bugs took my place.
These on top of the water where they play.
Now I use a kayak and on top of the water I stay.

Daffodil Hill

All that's green isn't clover, just cause it's cold
doesn't mean it won't get colder.
Just cause you fell into a hole doesn't mean
 the top won't close over.
If you traded it early without knowing the toll,
can it be taken back or is it too late?
Since all the rules you did break.
You made all the money, be it paper or coin.
Quarters and dimes seem so small unless
they're put in a roll.
Save it here to spend it there, can the lost
penny found,
be the one dropped by the beggar
on the other side of town?
Holding a sign with words that can't be read,
the moon in her eyes and a heart full of dread.
Have you ever slept under a bridge
with concrete for a bed?
Now and again, I think about the hitchhiker
and what he would do.
Thank you for the ride, being so grateful
that he's not you.

Passing Glance

Pass by each other without a glance
never mind a smile.
Don't dare look into the eyes for there
could be a friend within.
Why in such a hurry must we travel
with very few places to go?
One is to work, and the other is to play,
gone are the rules which we were taught in school.
I'll hold the door open if you can sit for a while.
Rest here for a moment, tell me of your chores.
Which do you cherish, and of which are you bored?
Tell me of your hopes then of the dreams that failed.
Tell me of the triumphs and of times spent
running the trails.
These are things I wish to know,
share your story let it be so.
Be it small steps or long leaps,
tell me all of what you heard.
Rest for a while then go upon your way.
Touch my hand for it has been a long day.
I can see the smile grow…
from that quick glance taken by chance.

December 17, 2023

Not Again

Time before and time again – time goes away
like grains of sand.
Yet sand remains – time is gone like water
in a holy bucket.
Rocks will crumble – stones will roll
– perhaps the holy water
will save your soul – read these words like
– the ones of old.
Behold the love we're afraid to let it show.
Rain in the winter fills the ditches, streams,
and rivers.
Which began to flow before the water
soaked to the aquifers below.
It's now in a hurry to leave taking with it
the sticks and branches, perhaps even the tree.
Don't need floods but sure welcome the rain.
Most we can do now is say,
"if the good lord's willing and the creek don't rise"
Too wet to plow – just right to hoe.
Rocks on top, good sandy loam below
– clay is full of minerals.
Which is a fact most folks don't know.

Southern Desert... est.2023

Nothing like a tornado that breaks and bends,
This was slow and deadly from beginning to end.
Pines stand brown – sick colored needles
cover the ground.
Arborvitaes stand as if dripped in brown glue.
Magnolias microwaved as the green
richness faded away.
Small shrubs planted early look
as if they were left in the toaster.
Sure, it was hot and yes it was dry
– no one saw it coming,
If they say they did - that's just a lie
– it moved in slow as a thief at nite.
Can only say as to what I saw
– the drought started it out.
Pine beetles soon took over like they were the law.
Knowing the rest of the work will be done with a saw.
Logs on the ground, cranes in the air,
spiders running around
like machines without a care,
stumps grinders finish out the day.
After a little raking it's time to collect the pay.
Dust blows, silt settles as the sun takes the water
from the clay.

Almost There

Coyotes roam… lap dogs stay at home.
Pages can turn yellow, and the words can fade.
If life flows thru the veins, these friends remain.
Not to be named, not to be famed,
ask no questions, be told no lies.
Hit and run away, to hit again another day.
Fun first, earth second, all for the cause yet not
knowing the way.
Just radicals in a hole with no place to go.
Taking trips at night hoping to return in the day.
Tempted to take another look for notes missed,
photos blurred,
can't finish the book if you've written not a word.
Read what you can, look between the lines.
Set aside the heartbreak of the post occupation blues.
All to do now is to continue the thread,
be the tip of the spear.
This was just one battle in what will be a lifetime war.
Lucky to have done any that we planned.
Grateful to those who fanned the flames.
So, the remaining pages will turn yellow,
words will fade.
The book is now finished and Al Most has fame.

Empty Before
Recycling
Bottle Not
Recyclable Unless
Label Removed
PLASTIC
BOTTLE
PLASTIC
LABEL
how2recycle.info

Drawing Water

Where does the new water come from?
Or has it always been there?
Tears from the stars, sprinkles from the comets.
Or is it filtered urine and morning vomit?
Will you drink from the stream or eat the snow?
Runoff from the fields and sprays
that increase the yield.
Kinda overwhelming how are we to feel?
Greenlighting makes it seem okay.
As corporations rape the planet
with promises of a better day.
Greta cries not alone as she carries the siren song,
Your house burns as you sit thinking
– no one must be home.
Bathe not in the Granges, bathe not in the Pearl.
Bathe where you dare…
the flesh-eating bacteria is already there.

Guerrilla Gardening Action...
to be continued

Take a barren red clay slope built by MDOT.
Spread organic debris and give this spot some hope.
Takes years of early mornings raids
just for any green to be seen.
Start with weeds then sow some seeds,
goldenrod and perilla.
Watching during a rain is hard to explain, down
floats the colored sand.
Where it builds a delta at the bottom of the slope.
Keep mulching gullies with leaves,
pine straw & hope…
Spiderwort begins to take root, cover them once.
After that it doesn't give a hoot.
Cannas and sunflowers struggle to make a display.
Wonder what the cut flowers folks would say.
Still filling the holes with anything that grows.
Not very pretty but that's how it goes…
Bermuda grass or Nandina berries,
not the best choices for me.
Yet it's either those or bamboo shoots
planted in rows.
Algae or a fern would be nice to see,
grow it up only to be mowed.
Keep composting and hope something takes hold.

The Wet Way

Crawling through fences, sleeping in ditches
while missing your home.
Headed into the unknown with barely a pig trail
to follow.
This trail became a road going north
to the other America they say.
What to do now, pay the fee or get lost along the way.
It's always been worth the trip;
generations have gone before.
Making a life of the work others can't or wouldn't do.
Amazing what a person will do if the choice
is up to you.
Carry them on your back, carry it in a sack,
barefooted or with shoes.
We talk of paying dues having no idea of these
modern traveler blues.
Sleep in the day, curry in the night, hoping for water,

if the stash location is right and the lids
were put on tight.
I've known men to work all week
then send home the wages.
Buying tractors for the farm
hoping the cartels go away.
Trains are the most dangerous,
one slip and a missed step
can lead to pain and often death.
Trash under the mesquite trees, kind of like
breadcrumbs back in the day.
Many are caught, some jailed in cages
makes no difference the
gender or the ages.

Earth Watch or Time Out

Easy to look past the issues
and where we went astray.
Was it at the game or while we watched others play?
Little by little, log by log, we cut the forests and
drained the bogs.
America the beautiful with straight roads
and tall glass buildings.
Replace the curves and brick shops with charging
stations and pit stops.
Billboards now all appear on screens,
don't text and drive.
Even your truck or SUV wants to survive
till the next day.
Wondering on its own then will it be traded away?
Robots without control
can start a business of its' own.
Corporations are now people is what the tax man say.

Continue in line to be fed the amount set aside today.
Then pick the numbers so ya can all feel
as if you got to play.
Cool breeze in the summer and warm when it's cold.
These are the vices that never grow old.
Take from a country for little or no pay.
Make it into something useless then throw it away.
Been doing this for a while resulting in trash
as part of the wind.
The arch of time has begun to bend
not knowing the effects.
Of mast production yet seeing where it could end.
As it's absorbed into the waters
and the mind melds of all.
Being lazy is fine when you see a short line.
But as the future grows in the children
and small trees.
We need to believe Earth is all we have
and all we need.

Peaceful War

Patterns were formed many centuries ago.
Where profits of war cast the light
of where we much go.
Ford the rivers and cut the trees, onward to
something never to show.
Peace has been shallow and murky at best.
Vision has been short yet to the moon we must go.
Mistaken as progress we reached without reward.
Cast the net into the sea, hauling up bottles
and bags of plastic!
A few shells or coral, mostly smooth glass, and
videos of the past.
Progress we reaped as low hanging fruit
then pulled up an old tire,
along with a fisherman's boot,
tangled in mono filament line.
Cutting to the bone any life it could find.
Needing to cast blame, wondering just the same.
Causes are many, reasons are few,
just go to worship on Sunday, what else can you do?
But pass the mess to the young,
hoping they'll be smarter
than me and you.
For making war is what we do.

Money Talks

As the sun warms the sky
and the trees cool the breeze.
Looking for answers without need of questions.
Here in the moment within the shadows
may you hide.
The early frost melts into dew,
drive to work, work to ride.
Saying what is wrong seems easier
than working to make it right.
The hypocrisy of our beliefs, the strength of your
faith can fill a bucket.
Or just empty your plate, now or later
doesn't really matter...
The shelves are empty, but the gardens remain full.
Warehouses are stacked with gadgets to be shipped.
Food deserts, abandoned malls, closed main streets
and that ain't all.
Rural hospitals in need of repair
as the smell of money fills the air.
What more to do... with a charlatan in the alley,
Crawling out of the mire, as a maggot becomes a fly,
Showing us again how easy it is to lie.
Half-truths have value in the weak of soul.
Money stirs the pot, but these coins are not gold.

WANTED!

Stories of Anti-Nuclear & Anti-War Resistance

Send the Nuclear Resister your story
about an arrest, courtroom experience,
or time behind bars.
Something inspiring or challenging,
humorous or surprising,
troubling or even transformative!

We will be using some, with
permission, to highlight the legacy
- and the continuing role -
of nonviolent direct action for a
peaceful, nuclear-free future.

*Send to nukeresister@igc.org
along with your name and contact
information. Thank you!*

Soul Prices

Torn from the land, cast into the city
without any pity.
Gone are the skills which helped us live,
replaced with a phone.
Always in touch, always on the roam,
headed downhill further from home.
If home is where the heart is then ours is at the bank.
Sleep in the suburbs, awake on the trains,
take trips on the web.
Not really knowing what to do,
hoping that all is good,
and no one shoots you.
Sad as it seems the goal is but a dream;
for the wealthy among us doesn't care.
All you can ask for was always there
until they sold the land ruining the plan.
Grow our own crops, saw our own wood
wasn't much to ask for.
Simply just trying to be good; foolish as it seems.
A lot of this remains in the scheme.
What will be made for the future?
What will be left after today's drones fly?
Who will write the answers
and who will question why?

Please do not...
Annoy
Criticize
Eat
Feed
Badger
Distress
Grab
Harass
Irk
Jinx
Kiss
Lasso
Maim
Nag
Oppress
Provoke
Ruffle
Quote
Scare
Tease
Undress
Vex
Yank
Zap
Wear
Xerox
...the animals.
Thanks!
ZOO
ZOO SAFETY HOTLINE
901-333-6677

Zoos

We put in the monkeys, then the kangaroos
along with the snakes.
Also, the birds that walked or flew next
to the largest plants which grew.
Built of stone with a few fences where the lost
orphans could roam.
A menagerie of animals that could roar and wale,
screech of the owl,
cry of the stolen, howl of the wolves
and the song of the whale.
It's beyond our ability as a species to understand
what they mean.
So, we feed them regularly and continue
with our saving schemes.
Lions, tigers, and bears walk around in circles,
swim in concrete ponds.
Never seeing the savannahs or the jungles again.
Born in captivity roaming the high fence safaris,
some be shot for a fee.
Most will lay in the shade eating chicken parts,
sleeping on hay.
Free the orcas, ocelots, ringtail cats and save the
Southern Plains Bumble Bee.

Bone Picker

With cows, horses, mules, dogs, cats,
and chickens one day they die.
Living in the country ya gotta realize this
or at least you ought to try.
Left in the field, dragged to the back corner,
to rot away.
Where the rats and the buzzards rule the night
and the day.
Bones for the picking and cow skulls for the wall.
Jawbone from a mule, looks handy,
makes quite a tool.
Only dug shallow graves sad to say which makes
good eating for the bugs.
Wished to be a gravedigger way back in the fray.
 Lure of coins or the jewelry… don't ask why cause
don't like to say…
Ended up a gardener and carrying a shovel every day.
Atonement for the past or payment for the future,
not to worry, not to fret started digging deeper holes.
Still haven't found the bottom yet.

IF I DIE IN A SCHOOl
SHOOTING LEAVE MY BODY
ON THE STEPS OF
CONGRESS

Current Protest in the Southeast

Gloster, Mississippi Drax wood pellet poison plant.
Memphis Byhalia pipeline right of way.
Louisiana Keystone XL pipeline issues
Atlanta… Stop Cop City
Rankin County… sheriff's goon squad.
Dallas air pollution…
Jacksons' water has always been unfit to drink.
One River No Lake… Save the Pearl
June 21, 2021… fire at Comanche Peak
Ball fields made of plastic; forests planted in rows.
No one knows where all the chemicals are buried or
when the barrels leak where this poison goes.
Single use items are our treasures today.
Use them once then throw them away.
Where is away, for these things last forever
not just for today?
The more we hear while wondering
about not being heard.
Yet the curse of our generation is eyes have we, but
we see not.
You know of all the wrong yet hardly ever speak of it.
As if the wrong will go away,
if we continue to have our say...

List

One day when my ashes become flowers.
And yours become a colony of butterflies…
Find me… I will be waiting.
Rain checks never bounce, can't afford your love
by the ounce.
Can pay by the year, once and again
as the dewdrops dry.
The rains began slowly with a sprinkle
then in a torrent.
Can't say for sure but a boat might this warrant.
Coming to explore what has been in front of me.
Eyes have I but still cannot see,
how far we have traveled.
Or why in an instant you went away.
Close but never near, yet at the Flowers
exit lost all the fear.
Just to speak once more, sit and listen to what
the rain has to say.
Gone again as the drama spins into
another River City day.
Never was sure if this was bliss
or the last item on my list?

Half a Hole?

Never seen half a hole… it's a mystery to me.
How a hole can be half the depth yet till a hole.
Divide it into half, it remains a hole.
Somethings I wonder about seem to be
a waste of time.
Yet it's the small things that clog the way
like picking up pennies,
while walking over dimes then throwing quarters
into a fountain
as if this will buy you more time.
While in haste throwing our resources away,
We've lost the wisdom of the past,
replacing it with holidays.
Where we must pay to play or give someone
colored paper.
Folded with care, taped at the corners
with a ribbon or bow.
Now that time is your friend, regift it all before
it becomes the foe.
Holes can be filled or can remain empty,
just as the search,
begins it will surely end with
or without a note or a song.
Half a hole cannot be just as a pond cannot be a sea.
Writing these words has helped me along.
As I walk in the dark in search of a spark.

Torn Again

Torn away from the love so freely given,
Mother from child.
As the hands lost their grip,
Slavery itself cursed the ship.
For the labor paid only in pain,
how do you give back after this?
No freedom paper or coin purse can repay
the damage only make it worse.
Some don't want to remember where
others refuse to forget.
Games of words and church choirs
sing old gospel hymns.
Too late for many, too early for the fools
that cast their thoughts,
with faith upon the waters which now boil for us all.
What was so violently torn away,
ripped from their homes.
Carrying only what they had on, memories,
scars and perhaps a song.
Laying in the hulls chained to themselves,
there's no way to know,
the pain and agony four hundred years
keeps wanting to show.
What can we do to right these wrongs,
reparations as requested?
"40 acres and a Mule" now seems as an insult
but it would have been a start.

Amortentia

Within the mist cloaking the lake weaves
a figure carrying a vial, here lies a potion.
Which dances in the early morning light
reflecting worry and delight.
From the shore all that is seen is the glass
heart shaped necklace she wears along with the vail.
Gifted before the flight as the fireflies
began their show.
Guiding them into the sky of a warm summer nite.
He reached for the necklace of jewels only to find
a string of fools hooked together
by the chain of time.
These were worn loosely to be easily cast away.
For she had been here shopping
and gathered them along her way.
He kept reaching ever so quickly,
still with no resolve.
No ruby nor pearl, all that was left
was a shell by the shore.
Colored blood red and engraved in gold
was a snapshot
of his life and grain of sand for his soul.
She appears with the dawn
as the violins of crickets' chirp.
He wonders about her notion and was all this
part of the potion?

Hymenocallis liriosme SPIDER LILY

Garden Talk

Into a garden I walked and to the asters I talked.
Most talked of themselves and of their time
in the sun.
One mentioned my name,
having heard this voice before.
I began edging closer wanting to hear more…
was distracted by a bee.
Looked around the garden as it was full of life,
with much to see.
More birds than flowers,
more trees than ants in a mound.
Turning this old pasture into a garden
healing the ground.
More will grow, more will follow if nature
can have her way.
Seedbanks will furnish the spores
along with the seeds.
We must be patient and sit under the trees,
enjoy the shade.
For it is truly the wealth to be found at no toll
only for the benefit of the earth
and our collective soul.

Tree Wages

The more I walked, the more the plants began to talk.
What else could you do other than plant a tree a day.
Large or small, oaks or elms, all these are worthy
of helping filter the air in town or country.
In the mornings when I awoke, some with coffee,
some with a toke.
There before me was a raging sea,
some called it a city.
Yet it was a torrent of cars in a whirlwind of roads.
Everyone swimming upstream
makes it a little uneasy.
Found it simpler to float, enjoying the ride
not taking sides.
Working for the wages yet yearning for something
of lasting for the ages… face the tree
and water the ring.
Prune the branches, remove the burlap and string.
Water once a week in the Texas heat,
mulch it with care.
Nobody else counted but I did this every day
for a year.

HOTEL TEXAS
FORT WORTH

Texas Time

Torn pages with words written with care,
Promises to change – lost to thin air.
Wrapped in lies so where to from there?
You're breaking my heart - you did this as a sport.
Did you buy or borrow what you've got?
Was just wondering so don't stare, do what you wish.
For what once was seen as a wink is now a glare.
Lit a candle when you entered the room,
funny it gives no light just a sense of doom.
Our bridges are now burnt by this flame.
Who hurts the most is the one that bears the blame.
You've now gone your way, as I struggle to speak.
The sound of your name will always make me weak.
If you wanted worship – why did you lie?
Your beauty that was, flew as a dove,
gone now having passed you by.
Satin are your dresses – silk are your slips.
You roared like a lioness as pain came from your lips.
So, roar not in my path as you sink passing ships.
Forever will you weep never to sleep.
Immortal throughout time will be
the hours you keep.

Boss Lady

Spring again turns the face of the South.
Brown with a million mounds of dirt,
touch not for it will hurt.
Once more ants can crawl up the stalks
to drink the dew.
Without the ice to slow the paths ants
march onward and thru.
Looking for something to chew,
take back to the mound.
Cut it into pieces then ferry it into the ground.
Tunnels and trails with yards to be crossed,
more drones for workers to feed,
along with a Queen always in need.
Her sisters are few, her servants are many,
her eggs are her crown.
All hail the Queens of the fire ant mound.
These can raft during a flood with every bite
it's going to sting.
Amazons of nature without any kings,
swarm in the spring.
New mounds a plenty, costing farmers
and ranchers a pretty penny.
Teach the kids to stay away, look where they step.
Or they will learn the hard way.

BLOW ON THIS DOT.
If It Turns Red, What The Government & Utilities Tell You About Nuclear Power, May Come True.
stonedwords & electric flowers
Jerry Palmer
Volumes 1-3
scan to visit website and to buy a copy of the book!

Write for You

Write for you any time of day,
always in thought of what to say.
Write for you yet can't remember your name,
saw you once
in a jewelry store, again in a garden
just before the rain.
Write for you wherever you might be,
lost in space or under a tree.
Write for you as the leaves change colors
and the sky remains blue.
No ones' fault but we must share the blame
not much glory,
in the endless walks of shame, as I write this story.
From the shadows of fires and the ladders of fame.
Write for you as I run to the flames,
shouting words as if I were sane.
Write to you, what else can I do?
Looked in all the gardens before and after the rains.
The flowers were cut and with the jewelry gone,
now what is left might just make a song.

Yards from Purple Creek

Having no streams flowing thru the woods,
what's a kid to do, can't go barefooted
cause of the trash.
Just build a golf course if you got the cash.
Nine holes or three, par fives or pitch and putt?
Only got creeks with the sides so steep,
help the privet thickets grow.
Fewer big gardens with rows to hoe,
now it's huge lawns with miles to mow.
Grass on the golf course mowed twice a day.
Want the front lawn to look the same way.
Putt from the roughs, lay up on the greens.
All seems natural but it's an alien dream.
Spray as needed and it's needed a lot.
Blue dye in the water, smoke in the air.
Dump it out back when there's nobody there.
Liquid stone to sharpen the reels,
just like the push mowers,
back in the day except these are in gangs cutting,
thin lines every which a way.

Wooden Posts

Cut and split from second growth trees,
rails spaced with wire.
Four or five strands is all that's needed
not much higher.
Stiles and gaps built and used to get across.
Hogs loose in the hills, wind blows
throughout the fields.
Be it cotton or growing beans,
fence posts were needed.
For on which the farmer to lean
and to keep the wild cattle at bay.
Osage orange was the tree of legend and of value.
Made into bows, buckets, and posts,
this was the tree planted the most.
Horse high, Bull strong and Pig tight,
none of these creatures could escape
no matter their fright.

Nailed with staples or wrapped in wire all the fences
to be stretched,
With crowbars and hammers now, the fences
are ten foot or higher.
Oak trees made good posts; cedar trees
now removed with dozers and chains.
Stacked and dried
from West Texas to the Hill Country
Horse apples, native pecan, prickly pear all free range
Hogs eat everything as if we're not there,
rooting up all the seeds.
Noses in the ground, tails in the air.
Trees for the taking, pines lost the most.
No one was looking – no one to toast.
When they turned the mighty oak
into a wooden post.

Empty Fish Bowl

No fish swim in your oceans, no gulls land
on your shore.
Tell me what happened,
and can they be replaced once more?
Tell me what you hold if not the dead sea
and a black oil soul.
Lotus are your beauty and crushed shells are the toll.
Fish bowls for the Betas, sand for the snails
and the marbles you roll.
Glass bowls are a gift, never shall they rust.
Carry them carefully for when they break
no water will they hold.
Small little ponds made of glass,
to swim in this bowl.
Is to live a life depending on others
and hoping the cat isn't bold.

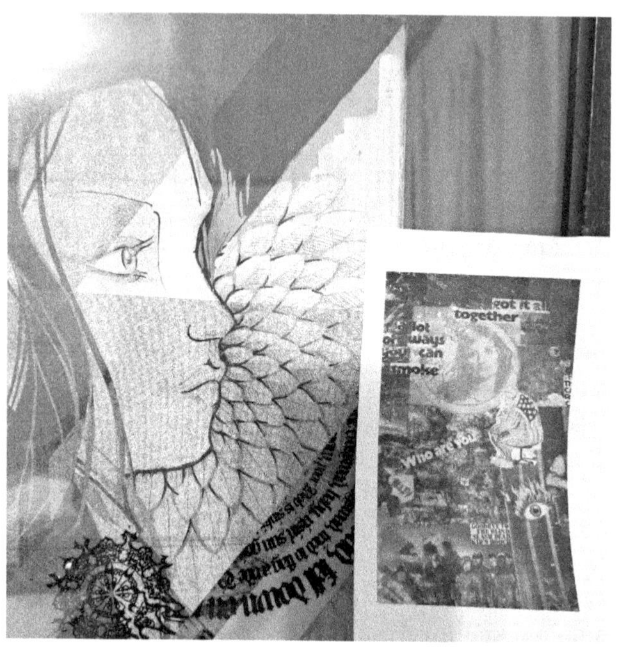
got it all
together
a lot
of ways
you can
smoke
Who are you
EDGY

Listening to You...
All I Want to Do...

I listened to your words – knowing not what to say.
Just what I heard, is it the blues
or are you always this way?
Many have written of this Lady – born of desire.
Lifelong journey reaching only to be higher.
She wore a heart of glass cast by the elves,
from the mountains of fire
on a chain of gold, linking this to our souls.
The ruby is missing nowhere to be found.
So, this is the end – all tomorrows will they say.
In looking for a silver platter,
he found but a bowl of clay.
Like roses upon the fence & zinnias in the yard.
Lost in the pages written for you
are all my wishes that came true.
With dried roses wrapped in twine & gifted charms
which cover this heart of mine,
while listening to you.

...THE
End